POETRY

for

GOD

JEAN MARIE PATTY

Published in the United States of America

Brilliant Books Literary
137 Forest Park Lane Thomasville
North Carolina 27360 USA

ISBN:
Paperback: 979-8-88945-431-1
Ebook: 979-8-88945-432-8

To my loving sister and best friend, Joan, and my other best friend, Janee. My sister took care of me for five months while I was very sick. She is so amazing! I love her dearly. She means everything to me. My sister is a very warm person and a wonderful caregiver.

I met my friend Janee because of my illness. I am so thankful that we became so close. She helped me see life in a whole new light because of her positive outlook. She is awesome!

ACKNOWLEDGMENTS

I would like to dedicate this book to my loving sister and best friend, Joan, and my other best friend, Janee! My sister took care of me for five months while I was very sick. She is so amazing! I love her dearly! She means everything to me! My sister is a very warm person and a wonderful caregiver!

I met my friend, Janee, because of my illness. I am so thankful that we became so close! She helped me see life in a whole new light because of her positive outlook! She is awesome!

I give all the glory to God above for giving me all the words for my poems! He is the greatest gift I have ever known!

God helped heal me from a very difficult illness. I love Him with all my heart and soul. I will always love Him, no matter what obstacles I may face.

I would like to thank my brother, Jim, for always being very supportive of my writing career. He is very special to me.

I want to thank my friend, Karen, for always supporting me in my artistic endeavors!

You are incredible and Your love for Jesus inspires me so much!

A very warm thanks goes to my friend, Donna, and her children, Aleah and Christian! They are all so wonderful and I love them very much!

A very special thanks to Nancie, Kelli, Rosemary, Jennifer, Judith, Ann, Kathryn, Vickie, Debbie, Susan, Brandy, and Ann-Marie! You are all so supportive and wonderful to me!

Thanks to all my other friends who love Jesus!

5

Last, but certainly not least, a very special thanks goes to my publisher, Brilliant Books Literary and especially to Amanda Spears!

Thanks also to Joey Scott and Jay Williams for all your hard work!

FOREWORD

First of all, I would like to say that I wrote this book because of my unfailing love for my King and Savior, Jesus Christ. He has provided me with so much happiness and autonomy. Without Jesus, I would have never been able to have found the words for these poems! Thank you, God, for all your blessings and gifts. You are so amazing and wonderful, and I love you with my whole heart!

I'm also thankful that you gifted me with my two precious kitties, Cream Puff and Evangeline. They do make my life complete!

Without your love, Lord, I am nothing!

I sincerely hope that anyone who reads this book will find true inspiration as my book was inspired by God.

HE IS THE LIGHT

He makes everything alright
Each and every night!
He is the most High
And He is the Light!

We're not worthy
of His sweet love
But He is amazing
And reigns from above!

Jean Marie Patty

9.03.23

*****

GOD GETS US THROUGH

It will all be okay;
God gets me through the day.
He holds the key and
He answers you and me.
God can always see and
we are set free.

Jean Marie Patty

9.20.23

*****

My Precious Princess

Evangeline is so loving
I just love her so!
She is so very cute
And that is all I know!

My kitty makes me happy
And makes me feel so fine!
She is so wonderful
And I feel sublime!

Jean Marie Patty

9.10.23

*****

My Love For Him Is Pure

The Lord is healing me
More and more each day!
He is good
In every single way!

He's helped me endure
And that is for sure!
He knows that my love
For Him is so pure!

Jean Marie Patty

9.05.23

*****

My New Life

I love my new life
Jesus is awesome!
He is always near
And I can blossom!

Jean Marie Patty

9.01.23

*****

My Sweet Janee

Thank You, precious Lord
For my sweet Janee!
Life would be empty
Without her for one day!

The Lord is kind
And knows what we need!
He is glorious and
He is beautiful indeed!

Jean Marie Patty

9.02.23

*****

I Love You, Puff

I wish you could
Live forevermore!
But you'll have to leave
And I'll be so bored!

I love you so much
You're everything to me!
You make me happy
And you set me free!

Jean Marie Patty

4.22.23

*****

Jesus Is Sweet

I love You, Jesus
Until the end!
You have always been
My sweet, precious friend!

For You are everything
You make me smile!!
I can't do without You
Even for a while!

Jean Marie Patty

5.01.23

*****

My Baby Sister

My baby sister is precious
I just love her so!
She is everything to me
I cannot let her go!

My sister takes care of me
And makes me feel complete!
She is so special to me
And keeps me on my feet!

Joan is a good mother
She knows how to deal!
She has learned tolerance
And she helps me to heal!

Jean Marie Patty

4.29.23

*****

GORTIE AND VANGIE

The babies love me
And I feel sublime!
They are precious
And they're all mine!

Jean Marie Patty

*****

VANGIE LOVE

I love Evangeline
So incredibly much!
She is very sweet
And soft to the touch!

Vangie is special
And always so true!
She makes me happy
I don't know what to do!

I love sweet Evangeline
For so many reasons!
I love her forever
And through all the seasons!

Jean Marie Patty

*****

GOD LOVES MY GIRL

God loves my precious baby
She is so very sweet!
She is wonderful
And so incredibly neat!

God loves her so
And wants her to live!
He gave her to me
So I could also save!

I give her love
Oh so very dear!
She loves me back
And she is always near!

Jean Marie Patty

4.26.23

*****

CREAM PUFF, I LOVE YOU

I'm going to miss you
It'll hurt like hell!
I love you so much
But all will be well!

For you will reign
In Heaven above!
With Jesus and the angels
And filled with sweet love!

I hate that you will
have to leave me!
I love you so much
But you will be free!

Jean Marie Patty

4.15.23

*****

KITTY LOVE

I love you, Gortie
As much as life!
But you're getting old
And it's causing me strife!

I wish you could
Live a whole lot longer!
But God will take you
When I am stronger!

I love you with
My whole wide heart!
You'll always be mine and
We're never far apart!

Jean Marie Patty

4.19.23

*****

I'm Going to Miss You!

No one melts my heart
The way that you do!
I love you forever
You are so very true!

I can't stand the thought
of being without you!
I am sad and scared
And so very blue!

I love you so much
I don't know what to do!
I wish you could stay
And I could be with you!

Jean Marie Patty

4.13.23

*****

My Love for Jesus

I love Jesus
Every single day!
I love Him so
In every way!

Jesus is truly
My very best friend!
And I will love Him
Until the very end!

For He is my Father
And I love Him so!
This much is true
I'll never let Him go!

Jean Marie Patty

*****

GLORIOUS JESUS

I want to be with Jesus
For all eternity!
For He is glorious
And gives me serenity!

Jean Marie Patty

5.14.23
Mom's Day!

*****

BLESSED

I'm so blessed
And full of happiness!
I have family, friends
And babies too!
They are all so true!

God is so awesome
Mighty and true!
He loves me and
He loves you!

Jean Marie Patty

5.09.23

*****

HE IS SO WONDERFUL

My sweet Lord
Is mighty, awesome and proud!
I want to sing
His praises out loud!

Jesus is good and true
And wonderful too!
He is always kind
And always on my mind!

Jean Marie Patty

*****

Our Lord Is Kind

I need your love
Through every single day!
I love you, Lord
Forever I will pray!

You are merciful
And so very kind!
You are everything
You're always on my mind!

I need your grace
To see me through!
For you are mighty
And awesome and true!

Jean Marie Patty

4.27.23

*****

HE IS EVERYTHING TO ME

God will always
Carry me through!
Because He is kind
And awesome and true!

I love my sweet Lord
So very much!
He is precious
And has a loving touch!

I will never leave Him
For He is my King!
He is so wonderful
And He is everything!

Jean Marie Patty

8.8.23

*****

Sing His Praises Out Loud

My Lord Jesus
Is awesome and proud!
I always choose to
Sing His praises out loud!

Jesus is merciful
And loving too!
He is wonderful
My love for Him is true!

Jean Marie Patty

*****

HE IS GRACE

I love my Lord
For He is good!
I love my Lord
I do what I should!

For I love Him
He is my saving grace!
He is merciful
And knows my name!

He is perfect
He makes me smile!
Will you please stay
If only for a while!

Jean Marie Patty

*****

YOU ARE EXTRAORDINARY

Lord, because of You
Being in my life,
There will certainly
Be a lot less strife!

The pain will be
Usually only temporary!
Because You are healing
And are always extraordinary!

You always help me
Through the troubled times!
You are so precious
And always on my mind!

Jean Marie Patty

*****

JESUS IS LOVE

I love Jesus so
He is all I know!
He is merciful
And the only way to go!

Jesus loves His children
And the animals too!
He is everything to me
And He should be to you!

For Jesus saved the world
With His unfailing love!
He is so mighty, yet
He is sweeter than a dove!

Jean Marie Patty

4.28.23

*****

Jesus Shows Us the Way

Do you feel overwhelmed?
Do you get sad and blue?
Look to the Lord
And He will guide you!

The Lord can show you
The error of your ways!
He will lift up your nights
And all of your days!

Jean Marie Patty

5.05.23

*****

HE CONSUMES

Life can sometimes
Seem so lonely!
But Look to Jesus
For He is the Only!

Jesus is the only
One who really cares!
He loves us all
And only He dares!

Jesus dares to love us
No matter how we act!
His love is all consuming
It's a matter of fact!

Jean Marie Patty

5.11.23

*****

GOD IS BEAUTIFUL

I know God helped
Me to walk again!
For He is good
And can do anything!

God has helped me
So very much!
He is wonderful
And has a mighty touch!

He is always kind
And so merciful!
He's been good to me
And He is beautiful!

Jean Marie Patty

5.08.23

*****

Through the Trials

Lord, help me to
Keep it all together!
For I am scared but
You are with me forever!

I am so afraid
And I feel so lonely!
I know you understand
You are the One and Only!

I need Your guidance
To carry me through!
I know You hear me
And You are so true!

Jean Marie Patty

4.17.23

*****

He Is the Almighty

He did it for us
Jesus died on a cross!
He will live forever
Without Him, we are lost!

Jesus is the greatest
He died for you and me!
Jesus is the Almighty
He will set us free!

Jean Marie Patty

5.03.23

*****

HE IS MERCIFUL

Our Lord is sweet
And reigns up above!
He is awesome and
Is filled with great love!

I love Jesus
All of the time!
He is merciful
And He is mine!

Mine for the asking
And always good!
He is mighty and
We are understood!

Jean Marie Patty

5.03.23

*****

Jesus Is Awesome

I live for Him
He is so very strong!
Without my Jesus
I cannot carry on!

I want to live
For Jesus alone!
He is awesome
And He is my home!

Jean Marie Patty

5.04.23

*****

HIS LIFE HE GAVE

Nobody but Jesus
Makes me feel such love!
He is the greatest
He reigns up above!

The face of Jesus
Is all that can save!
We are His children
And His life He gave!

Jean Marie Patty

5.05.23

*****

HE KNOWS ME

I'm feeling better
After some sleep!
I pray to the Lord
My soul to keep!

He gets me through
The bad times and good!
He is so awesome
I'm always understood!

I need His guidance
To help me through!
He knows me well
And He is so true!

Jean Marie Patty

5.01.23

*****

He Always Loves

You never change
You remain the same!
You always have
An unfailing name!

You are mighty,
Awesome and true!
And I will always
Forever love You!

For You are good
And so very kind!
You are perfect and
The most wonderful find!

Jean Marie Patty

5.02.23

*****

HE IS GOOD

He takes my
sin and shame away!
He is just perfect
In every single way!

He is awesome,
Powerful and true!
He loves me and
He loves you!

He will forgive
And set you free!
He is in everything
And He is good to me!

Jean Marie Patty

5.02.23

*****

WE ARE SENT FROM ABOVE

God always makes me
Feel so fine!
He is awesome
And blows my mind!

The Lord is kind
And so beautiful!
I love Him so much
I long to be dutiful!

God is gracious
And worthy of love!
He reigns in Heaven
We are sent from above!

Jean Marie Patty

4.29.23

*****

GOD IS GRACIOUS

I know God loves me
I try to be nice!
He loves His children
He doesn't think twice!

God loves everyone
Even when were wrong!
He always forgives
We praise Him in song!

God is gracious
And loving and kind!
He is so sweet
He's always on my mind!

Jean Marie Patty

5.08.23

*****

Jesus Is Kind

He is trustworthy
And He is kind!
Jesus will always
Be on my mind!

For I love Jesus
Always and forever!
He is amazing
And He is my Savior

Jesus is a giver
of love and grace!
I always long to see
His beautiful face!

Jean Marie Patty

*****

Jesus Is Faithful

I know this to be true
I do truly love You!
You are my everything
You make me want to sing!

Jesus will never change
He always stays the same!
He is so powerful
And He knows my name!

My sweet precious Lord
Is always so faithful!
He is kind
And so very beautiful!

Jean Marie Patty

*****

You Are Perfect

Jesus, I love You and
You are my everything!
I praise Your name
You make my heart sing!

Jesus, You are so kind
And loving and true!
You are perfect
And I love You!

Jean Marie Patty

*****

OUR HEALING LORD

Lord, please help Jennifer
I know that You can!
You are always near
You will hold her hand!

For You are the guiding light
That always gets us through!
You are surely able
And You know what to do!

Jean Marie Patty

*****

I Love Him Completely

I love to rhyme
All of the time!
God is awesome
And He is mine!

Jesus is the reason
For all that we do!
I love Him completely
He always sees me through!

Jean Marie Patty

*****

GIVE GOD THE GLORY

I give all the glory
To God up above!
For He is awesome
And filled with great love!

He helps me to write
And lets me create art!
He is so wonderful
From the very start!

Jean Marie Patty

*****

PUFF AND EVANGELINE

Cream Puff is fine
And she's all mine!
I love her so and
I'll never let her go!

Vangie is beautiful
And so very sweet!
She is just lovely and
Is a special treat!

I love them both
Much more than life!
They're both awesome
And never cause strife!

Jean Marie Patty

9.03.23

*****

JESUS IS GOOD

I love Jesus
because He is good.
He is awesome
and I'm always understood.

Jean Marie Patty

*****

AMAZING GRACE

Gracie is sweet
and she is funny too.
She does my heart good
and that is so true.

Gracie loves my babies
and that means everything.
She is so precious and
she makes my heart sing.

Jean Marie Patty

*****

PRECIOUS JANEE

My sweet and loving Janee
always makes my day.
She is so precious
in every single way.

I think she is awesome
and so very kind.
She is a lot of fun
and simply blows my mind.

I hope that we become
the very best of friends,
because I'll always care
until the very end.

Jean Marie Patty

*****

My Friend Janee

Janee and I met
because I was in pain.
We really hit it off
and there is more to gain.

We have a lot in common
and we love to share.
Janee is so precious
and I will always care.

God brought us together
so that we could truly see,
that everything will be alright
and we can be set free.

I truly adore Janee
because she is so kind.
To think of life without her
would simply blow my mind.

Jean Marie Patty

*****

OUR REDEEMER

My Jesus is perfect and
that is what I know.
He is our Redeemer and
I let my love for Him show.

Jesus answers my prayers
and He is always kind.
He always forgives and
He never leaves my mind.

Jean Marie Patty

*****

My Friend Ann

Ann is a lovely person
and also she is kind.
She is very special
and is always on my mind.

Ann loves the Lord
and sings His song.
We talk of Jesus
and we share for so long.

I love sweet Ann
with all my heart.
She is my friend and
we're never far apart.

Jean Marie Patty

*****

Janee Is Sweet

Lord, let my friendship
with Janee grow and grow!
I love her so much
and cannot let her go!

Janee is so sweet
and so very neat!
She is really funny
and that you can believe!

Jean Marie Patty

*****

HE IS MY SWORD

I will never be ashamed
of my love for the Lord!
For He is kind to me
And He holds the sword!

The sword is His strength
And He gives it to me!
He helps me with strife
And He will set me free!

Jean Marie Patty

9.06.23

*****

I NEED JESUS

Jesus, I want You so
You are so very true!
You have blessed me
And I love You!

You are generous
And so very kind!
You are in my heart
And always on my mind!

You are everything to me
I'll never let you go!
I need You so much
And that is what I know!

Jean Marie Patty

9.11.23

*****

HE IS KIND

I need the Lord
In my life!
He always keeps me
Far from strife!

When I'm feeling down
I ask Him for relief!
He always listens
And cares beyond belief!

For the Lord is good
And knows my name!
He is forever kind
And remains the same!

Jean Marie Patty

9.02.23

*****

I Love God

God is kind and
Merciful and true!
He healed me when
I didn't know what to do!

He is mighty, awesome
And proud!
I love Him so much;
I sing His praises out loud!

Jean Marie Patty

9.01.23

*****

Stay with Me

I love You, Jesus
So very much!
You are kind and true
With a sweet gentle touch!

You make me happy and
You make me smile!
I know You will always
Stay for a long while!

Jean Marie Patty

9.02.23

*****

JEAN MARIE PATTY

He Always Knows

Jesus is so kind
He helps me through!
He always knows
Just what to do!

I love You, God
For You are holy!
I am always Yours
And You are the only!

You are the only One
Who can help me see!
That it will be alright
And You will never leave!

Jean Marie Patty

*****

HE IS FIRST IN MY LIFE

Jesus, You are everything to me
That's the way it'll always be!
Because I love You so much
You have a sweet and precious touch!

You make me feel fine
You will always be mine!
Jesus, You keep me from grief
In You, I always find relief!

Jesus, You keep me from strife
You are always first in my life!
I love You forever!!

Jean Marie Patty

*****

Jesus Is Glorious

I know this to be true
This is my reality!
You are my whole life
And You provide tranquility!

You give me sweet love
All of the time!
I am yours always
And You are all mine!

Stay with me forever
And never leave my side!
You are everything to me
From You, I cannot hide!

I can't hide from Your love
For You are glorious!
I will always love You
And You remain victorious!

Jean Marie Patty

*****

My Beautiful Cream Puff

I love you so much
My beautiful baby girl!
You are my life
And my whole wide world!

I love you each day
You are so very grand!
You are truly wonderful
And the best in the Lord!

My sweet love for you
Is incredibly pure!
I love you forever;
of that you can be sure!

Jean Marie Patty

4.13.23

*****

JEAN MARIE PATTY

God Is Always Good

The Lord had always
done great things.
He is awesome and
makes my heart sing.

I love the Lord
with all of my heart.
He is always good
right from the start.

Jean Marie Patty

*****

I Sing Your Praises

I praise Your holy name, Lord
for you are everything.
With You in my life,
I want to dance and sing.

I sing Your praises
for You are good.
You are mighty and
I'm always understood.

You know my name and
You help me with my pain.
You are merciful and
You keep me sane.

Jean Marie Patty

*****

FRIENDS

I love Ann
and Willie Mae.
They are sweet
and make my day.

Ann and Willie are nice
and they are so kind.
I just adore them and
they blow my mind.

Jean Marie Patty

*****

BEAUTIFUL JOAN

My sister is so sweet and
I just love her so.
She is everything to me and
I cannot let her go.

My sister takes care of me
and helps me feel alright.
She's beautiful inside and out.
She is never far from sight.

Joan helps me to heal and
she is so special to me.
Joan is a wonderful person.
She lets me feel so free.

Joan is so funny and
cute as can be.
She always makes me laugh
and fills my heart with glee.

Jean Marie Patty

*****

My Sister, Joan

Joan is my best friend and
I love her to the end.
She is good to me and
helps set me free.

My sister is so very
sweet and kind.
She is a wonderful find and
is always on my mind.

Jean Marie Patty

*****

You Are Faithful

Lord, please don't put
too much on me.
I get so afraid and
I also get lonely.

I know You hear me
when I call Your name.
You are so faithful and
You always keep me sane.

Jean Marie Patty

*****

LIFE IS DIFFICULT

It's a vicious cycle
that leads to despair,
but look to the Lord
as He will be there.

Never give up hope
for God is so good.
Life can be difficult
but we are always understood.

Jean Marie Patty

*****

GOD LOVES ME

The stupid enemy
tries to get to me,
but God is healing
and sets me free.

God helps me to see
that all will be okay,
and He will love me
forever in a day.

Jean Marie Patty

*****

I WILL BE ALRIGHT

The trials were horrible and
I didn't know what to do,
but my love for Him endured
and this much is true.

I thought I would die,
but it wasn't my time.
He helped me go on and
then I was just fine.

I'm not completely healed and
I've got a long way to go.
But God is so loving
and He always lets it show.

Jean Marie Patty

*****

PRECIOUS DONNA, ALEAH AND CHRISTIAN

Donna is my friend and
I love her to the end.
She is so very kind and
she always blows my mind.

Donna teaches me to paint as
she is so very smart.
She means the world to me.
I loved her from the start.

I love Donna's children
because they are so sweet.
Aleah and Christian are wonderful.
They knock me off my feet.

Jean Marie Patty

*****

HIS KIND WAYS

I choose to pray
all of the time,
because I know that
He is all mine.

He gets me through
the darkest of days.
I love the Lord and
all of His kind ways.

Jean Marie Patty

*****

I Place My Heart with God

It's a new day
and a fresh start.
Where do you want
to place your heart?

We should place it in
the loving faith of God.
Yes, He is awesome and it's
really not that odd.

Jean Marie Patty

*****

MY FRIEND KATHRYN

Kathryn is my good friend.
We go back a long way.
She is very kind and
she just makes my day.

Kat is very talented and
loves cats like I do.
She is something special
and that is so very true.

Jean Marie Patty

*****

My Precious Karen

Karen is my dear friend
and she is very kind.
I love her so much;
she is a wonderful find.

Karen helps me get better
when I am feeling sad.
She is always healing
and she never gets mad.

I adore my precious Karen.
She is so very sweet.
She is my special friend and
she is an awesome treat.

I need Karen in my life.
She is so very dear.
I always think of her and
she is always near.

Jean Marie Patty

*****

You Are the Greatest

Lord, I need you
every single day.
I love You so much
and I will always pray.

I am especially sad
about my sweet Puff,
but Your love is pure
and is always enough.

I love You so much
with all of my being.
You are the greatest and
You are always worth seeing.

Jean Marie Patty

*****

JESUS UNDERSTANDS

I have to be discerning
as I am always yearning
to do my very best.
He puts me to the test.

I try hard for Jesus
and He always understands.
For I am not perfect,
but He always holds my hands.

Jean Marie Patty

*****

HE IS GREAT

Lord, please help me
as I am afraid.
I need Your guidance and
all that you've made.

Your glory and goodness
are just what I need.
I love You forever and
You are great indeed.

Jean Marie Patty

*****

GOD IS PRECIOUS

Lord, You are kind and
You never fail me.
You are so precious,
but I am not worthy.

You answer my prayers
and You never leave.
You are extremely awesome
and I truly do believe.

Jean Marie Patty

*****

HE REIGNS ABOVE

I love my precious God
with all of my heart.
He has been amazing
right from the start.

I cannot live without
God's everlasting love.
He is the almighty and
He reigns from above.

Jean Marie Patty

*****

MY BEST FRIEND IS JESUS

I love my sweet Jesus
all of the time.
He is my Savior and
forever He is mine.

I love Him so much
until the end of time.
Jesus will always be
a true friend of mine.

Jean Marie Patty

*****

My Dear Friend Nancie

Nancie is my dear friend
She is so very kind.
I love her to pieces and
she just blows my mind.

Nancie is supportive of all
of my endeavors.
She is so smart and
is really quite clever.

Nancie means the world to me;
I just adore her so.
She is very loving and
she certainly seems to glow.

Nancie has a love for the Lord
that is so very inspiring.
She is just awesome
and so worth admiring.

Jean Marie Patty

*****

THE WORDS ARE FREEING

Writing is an outlet
that just sets me free.
I love it every day
and that you can believe.

God gives me the words
for He is all knowing.
I worship Him always
and He is just glowing.

Jean Marie Patty

*****

Peace in Writing

Writing is quite often
a rather cathartic release.
I enjoy it so much;
it brings me such peace.

Jean Marie Patty

*****

My Friend Kelli

Happy birthday, Kelli.
I love you so.
You are precious and
that is all I know.

You are a child of God.
Your faith encourages me.
You are my true friend.
You fill my heart with glee.

I have loved you
for such a long time.
You are so special and
a dear friend of mine.

Jean Marie Patty

*****

THE JOY OF WRITING

How I love to write
every single night.
It's a form of expression
that keeps me from suppression.

Jean Marie Patty

*****

Autonomy

God changed my life drastically
and gave me autonomy.
He is our Creator and
He is everything to me.

Jean Marie Patty

*****

I LOVE MY SISTER

My sister is kind
and often misunderstood.
She's got a heart of gold
and she tries to do good.

I love my sister
so very much.
She's my best friend and
we love to talk and such.

Jean Marie Patty

*****

About the Author

Jean Marie Patty was raised in Anniston, Alabama. She has also lived in California, Florida, New Hampshire, and Atlanta. She studied at Florida State University and loved writing and art courses. She also loves photography. She loves God, family, friends, and her cats.

Jean Marie hopes that all who read her book will find inspiration.

BACK COVER SUMMARY

Jean Marie wrote this book during some very difficult trials. She always relied on God for her healing. Her book is about God first then family, friends, and her two cats. She loves all these with her whole heart and soul.